OFFICIAL

Updated
Second Edition

T0373831

Kid's Box

Starter Class Book

with **CD-ROM**

British English

Caroline Nixon & Michael Tomlinson

Language summary

1 Hello!

1 **CD1** 2 Listen and point.

2 **CD1** 3 Say the chant.

4

3 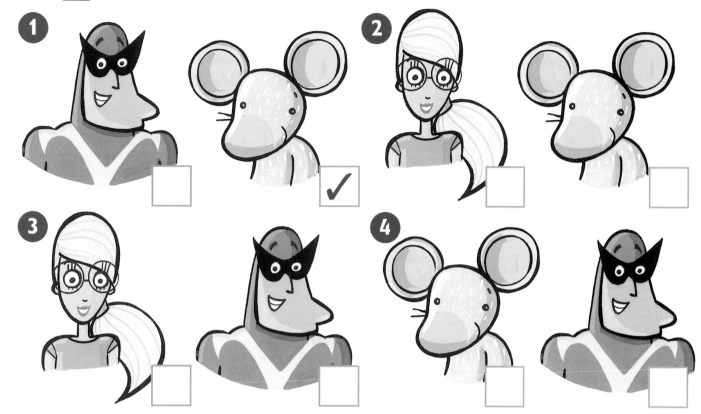 🎵 ✏️ Listen and tick (✓).

4 🔍 ✏️ Look and draw. Say the number.

Marie   Maskman   Monty   one   two   three   What's your name?   I'm ...

6  Look and draw. Say the numbers.

2	••
6	
3	

5	
1	
4	

7 Listen and circle.

1
2
3
4

8 Listen to the story.

1

2

3

4

5

6

9  **Listen and stick.**

10 **Talk to Maskman.**

?

2 My class

1 11 CD1 Listen and point.

2 12 CD1 Say the chant.

3 🔊 CD1 ✏️ Listen and circle the number.

1

4 (5)

2 2 3

3 3 4

4 2 3

5 5 6

6 1 2

4 🔍 ✏️ Look and complete.

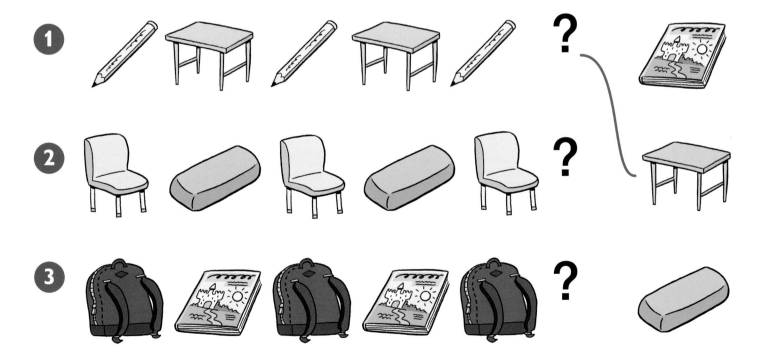

1 ?

2 ?

3 ?

bag book chair eraser pencil table   **11**

5 14 CD1 Listen and point. Sing the song.

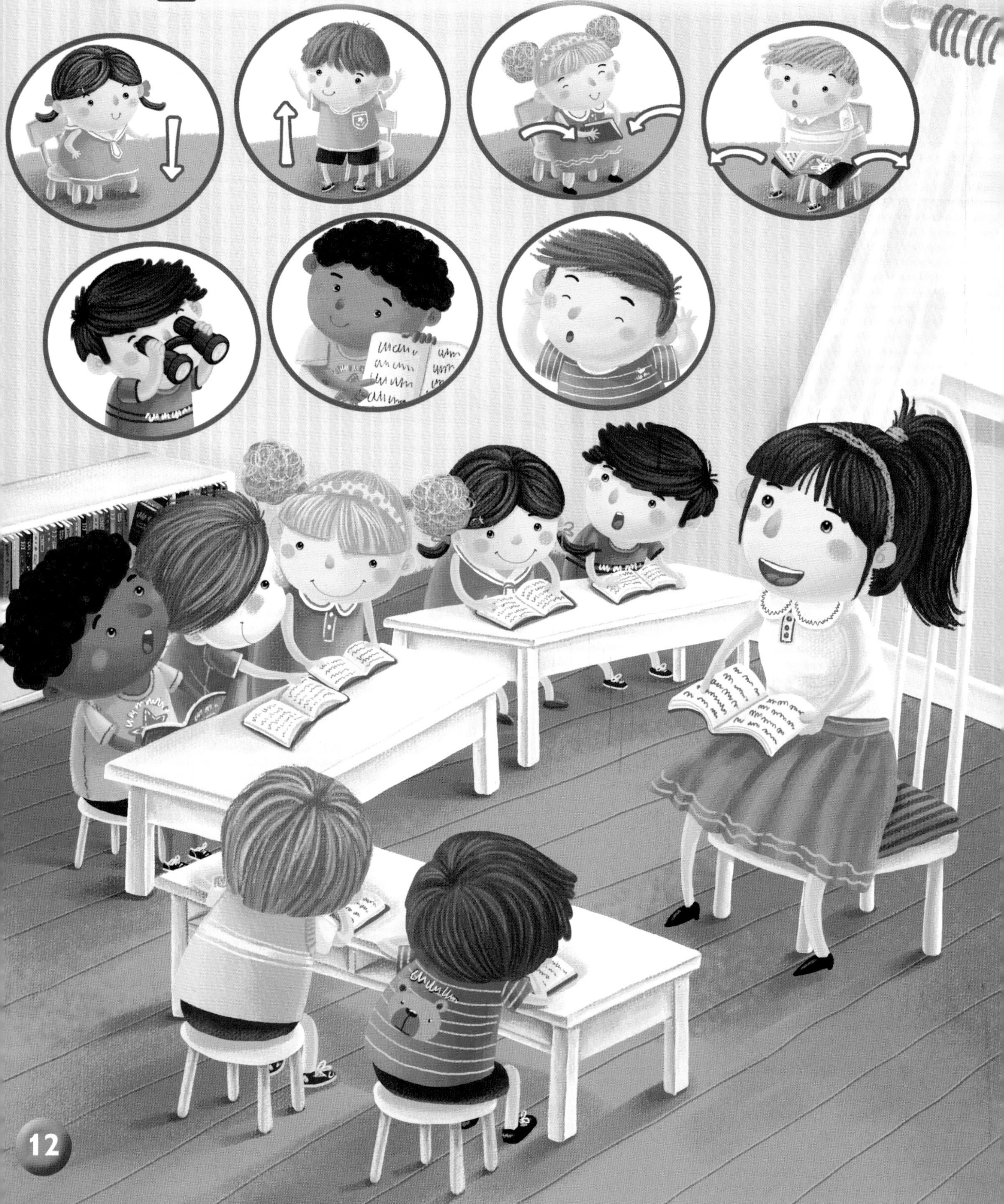

7 Draw your classroom. Say.

Me!

open your books   close your books   stand up   sit down   listen   look   point

13

9 🔢 18 CD1 👶 Listen and stick.

1

2

3

4

5

6

10 🔢 19 CD1 💬 Talk to Maskman.

?

1  Listen and point. Say the chant.

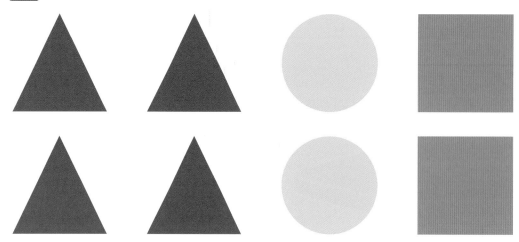

2 Look and count. Make and say.

3 **21** CD1 Listen and point.

4  Act it out.

Pass me the ... please.   Here you are.   Thank you.   **17**

3 My colours

3 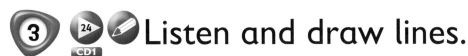 **Listen and draw lines.**

1 **2** **3**

4 **Listen and colour.**

1
2
3
4
5
6

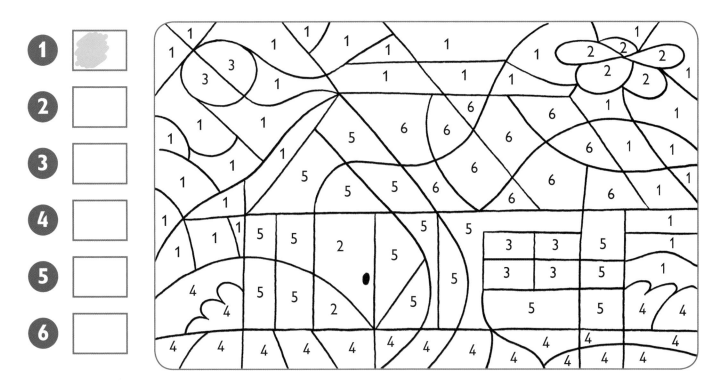

black   blue   brown   red   white   yellow

6 **28** CD1 Listen and colour.

1 2 3

4 5 6

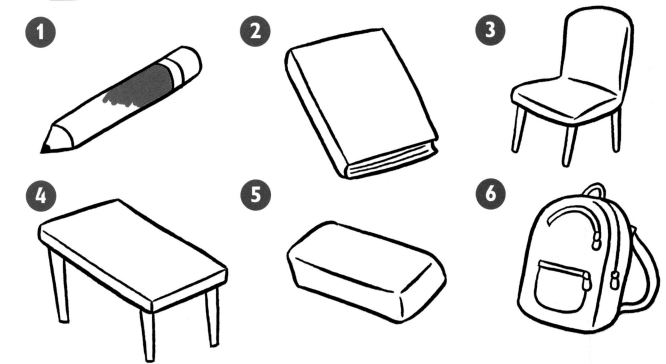

7 **29** CD1 Listen, count and answer.

It's red.   It's a red pencil.

8 ▶30 CD1 Listen to the story.

9  Listen and stick.

1

2

3

4

5

6

10 Talk to Maskman.

?

4 My toys

1 33 CD1 Listen and point.

2 34 CD1 Say the chant.

3  **Listen and colour.**

4 **Listen and draw lines.**

ball   bike   car   doll   kite   robot   **25**

5 🔊 37 CD1 🎵Listen and point. Sing the song.

26

6 Listen and write the number.

7 Draw your favourite toy. Say.

Me!

Listen to the story.

9 🔊 **41** CD1 👤 Listen and stick.

1

2

3

4

5

6

10 🔊 **42** CD1 💬 Talk to Maskman.

?

1 🔍✏️ Look and draw lines.

2 🤸💬 Make a butterfly. Say the colours.

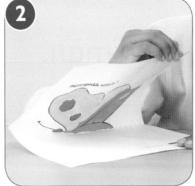

orange   green   pink

3 Listen and point.

1

2

3

4

4 Act it out.

Review

1 🔊 44 CD1 ✏️ Listen and circle the number.

1  ⑤ 6

2  2 3

3  3 4

4  1 2

2 🔊 45 CD1 ✏️ Listen, count and colour.

1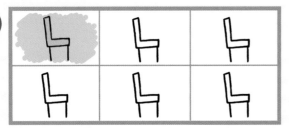

2

3

4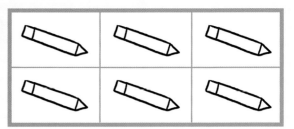

5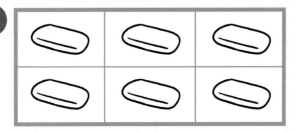

6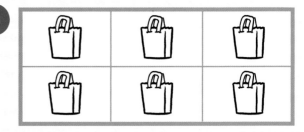

3 🔊46 CD1 ✏️ Listen and colour.

1

2

3

4

5

6

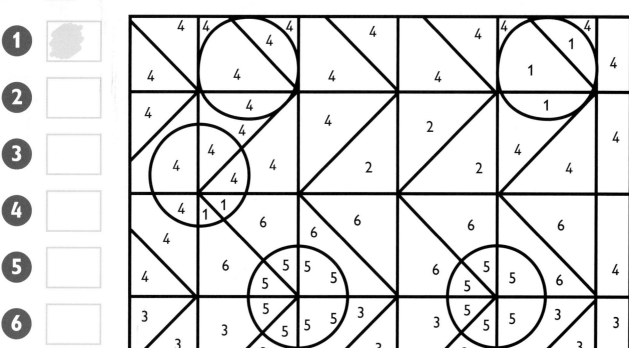

4 🔊47 CD1 ✏️ Listen and write the number.

1

5 My house

1  CD2 Listen and point.

2 CD2 Say the chant.

34

3  Listen and circle.

4 Listen and colour.

bedroom   kitchen   living room   bed   door   sofa   **35**

6 **8** CD2 Listen and draw lines.

7 **9** CD2 Listen and follow.

in   on   under   He's ...   She's ...   **37**

Listen to the story.

9 🔊11 CD2 👤 Listen and stick.

1

2

3

4

5

6

10 🔊12 CD2 💬 Talk to Maskman.

?

39

6 My body

2 **14** CD2 Say the chant.

40

3 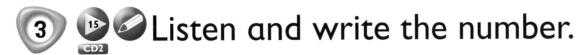 **Listen and write the number.**

4 **Look and complete.**

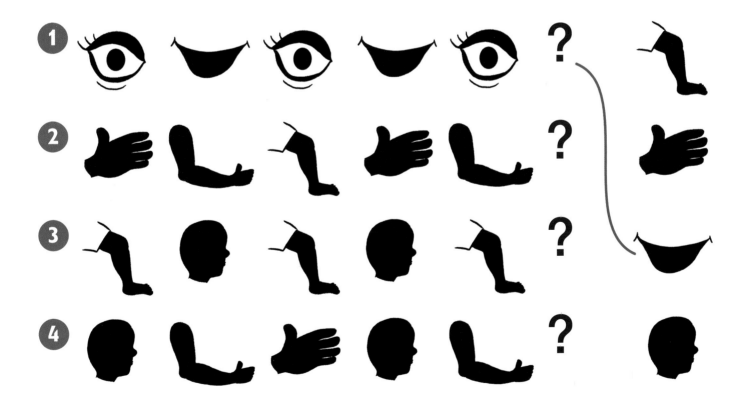

arm   eye   hand   head   leg   mouth

5 16 CD2 Listen and point. Sing the song.

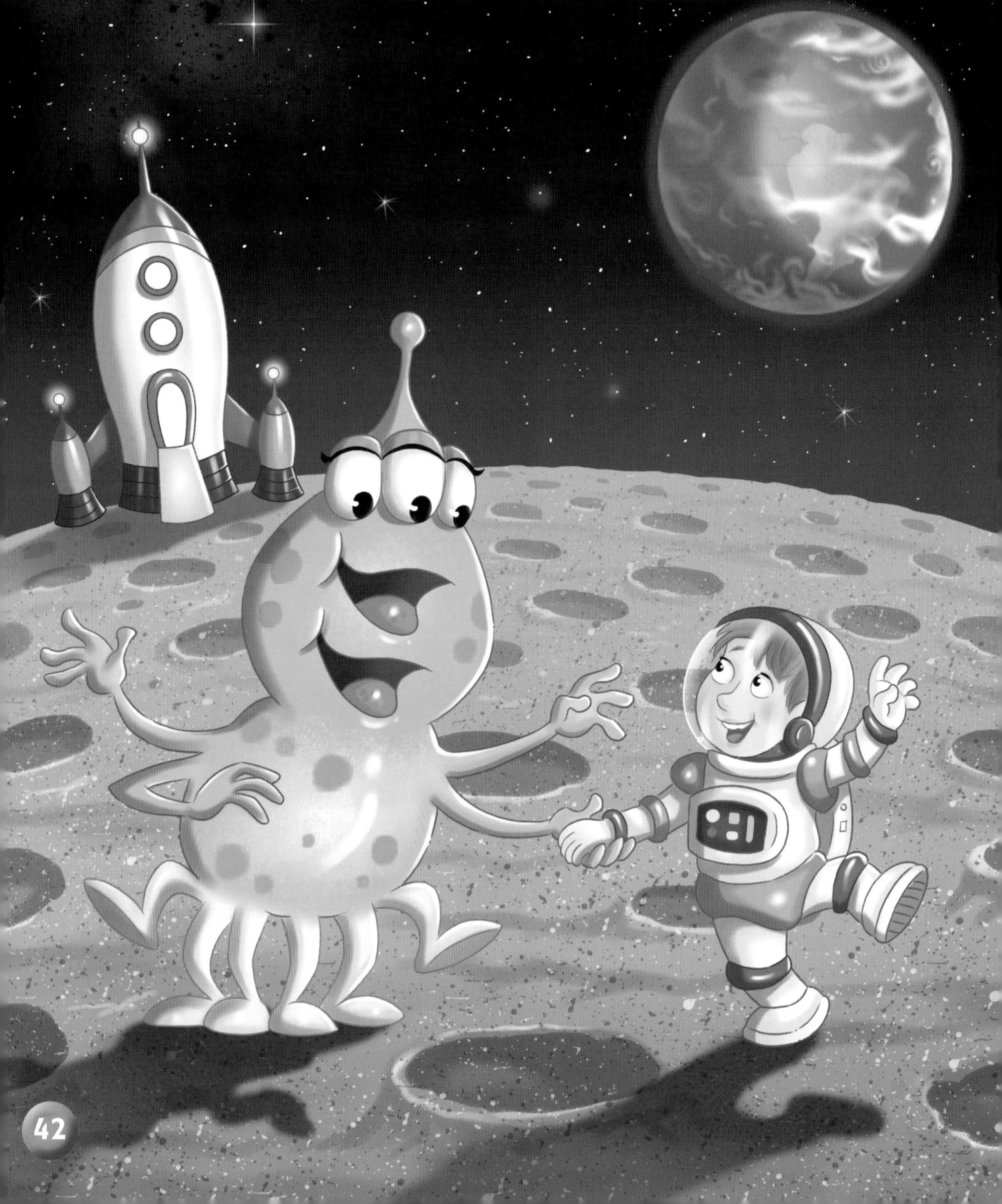

6 🔢 18 CD2 ✏️ Listen and tick (✓).

7 ✏️💬 Draw an alien. Say.

Me!

8  Listen to the story.

9 **20** CD2 Listen and stick.

10 **21** CD2 Talk to Maskman.

1   Listen and write the number.

2 Make a book. Say.

house tree wood

3  Listen and point.

1

2

3

4

4 Act it out.

Let's play pairs.   OK.   You start.   It's my turn.   **47**

7 My animals

1 🔊24 CD2 👆 Listen and point.

2 🔊25 CD2 💬 Say the chant.

48

3 26 CD2 ✏️ Listen and follow.

4 27 CD2 ✏️ Listen and draw lines.

bird dog duck fish frog tiger

6 **(30)** CD2 🖊 Listen and tick (✓).

1

2

3

4

7 **(31)** CD2 🖊 Listen and write the number.

1

I can ...   I can't ...   fly   jump   swim   **51**

9 🔊 33 CD2 Listen and stick.

10 🔊 34 CD2 Talk to Maskman.

8 My food

1 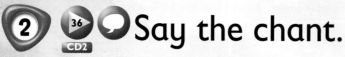 Listen and point.

2 Say the chant.

3  Listen and circle.

4 Look and complete.

56

6 🎧40 CD2 ✏️ Listen and write the number.

7 ✏️💬 Draw foods you like and don't like. Say.

Me! ✔

Me! ✗

8 **41** CD2 Listen to the story.

Listen and stick.

1 2 3

4 5 6

10 43 CD2 Talk to Maskman.

 **?**

1 🔊 44 CD2 ✏️ Listen and write the number.

2 👥 💬 Make a poster. Say.

frog's eggs   tadpole   water

3 Listen and point.

4  Act it out.

Review

1 🔊46 CD2 ✏️ **Listen and draw lines.**

2 🔊47 CD2 ✏️ **Listen and circle.**

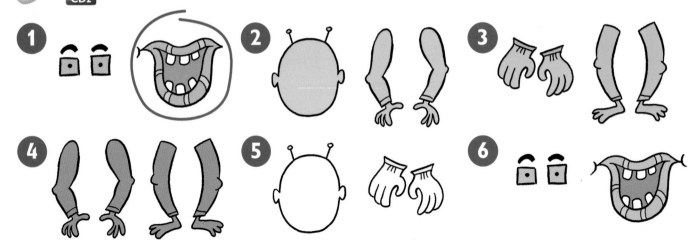

3  **Listen and colour.**

4 49 CD2 ✏ **Listen and draw lines.**

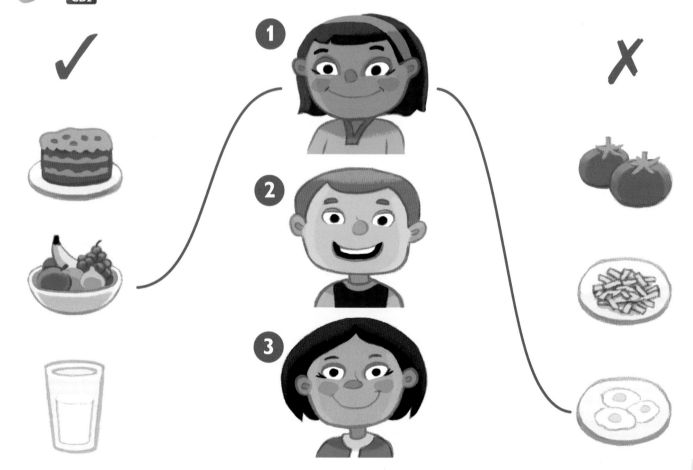

Thanks and Acknowledgements

Authors' thanks

Many thanks to everyone at Cambridge University Press and in particular to:

Rosemary Bradley for supervising the whole project and using her fine organizational skills to bring it all together;

Colin Sage for all his hard work, enthusiasm, keen eye for detail and invaluable input;

Emily Hird for getting the ball rolling and overseeing the development of the project;

Susan Norris-Roberts for coming back on board with her professional experience, expertise and invaluable advice.

Dedications

To Lydia and Silvia, with all my love. CN

To Paloma. Thank you for all your love, help and support along the way. MT

The Authors and Publishers would like to thank the following teachers for their help in reviewing the material and for the invaluable feedback they provided:

Russia: Irina Polyakova, Lyceum Stolichny; Zahra Bilides, Language Link. Turkey: Ebru Vural and Nural Edizsoy, Maya Koleji; Maria Topkar, Çevre Private School.

We would also like to thank all the teachers who allowed us to observe their classes, and who gave up their invaluable time for interviews and focus groups.

The authors and publishers acknowledge the following sources of copyright material and are grateful for the permissions granted. While every effort has been made, it has not always been possible to identify the sources of all the material used, or to trace all copyright holders. If any omissions are brought to our notice, we will be happy to include the appropriate acknowledgements on reprinting.

p. 17 (background): Thinkstock; p. 30 (pink & blue butterfly): Shutterstock/suns07; p. 30 (orange butterfly): Shutterstock/Sari ONeal; p. 30 (green & red butterfly): Shutterstock/Aleksandr Kurganov; p. 31 (background): Thinkstock; p. 46 (tree): Shutterstock/Le Do; p. 46 (logs): Shutterstock/koya979; p. 46 (table): Shutterstock/Chukcha; p. 46 (door): Shutterstock/YK; p. 46 (house): Shutterstock/bioraven; p.46 (bed): Shutterstock/sagir; p. 46 (chair): Shutterstock/Chamille White; p. 17 (background): Thinkstock; p. 60 (frog spawn): Shutterstock/DJTaylor; p. 60 (tadpole): DP Wildlife Vertebrates/Alamy; p. 60 (frog): Shutterstock/Matthijs Wetterauw; p. 61 (background): Thinkstock.

Commissioned photography on pages 16, 30B, 46B, 60B by Trevor Clifford Photography.

The authors and publishers are grateful to the following illustrators:

Beatrice Costamagna, c/o Pickled ink; Chris Jones; Helen Naylor, c/o Plum Pudding; Kelly Kennedy, c/o Sylvie Poggio; Melanie Sharp, c/o Sylvie Poggio; Richard Hoit, Beehive; Xian Xio, c/o Illustrationweb

The publishers are grateful to the following contributors:

Louise Edgeworth: picture research and art direction
Wild Apple Design Ltd: page design
Blooberry: additional design
Lon Chan: cover design
Melanie Sharp: cover illustration
John Green and Tim Woolf, TEFL Audio: audio recordings
Robert Lee, Dib Dib Dub Studios: song writing and production
hyphen S.A.: editorial management